MEAN MACHINES

RACING CARS

MARK MORRIS

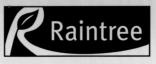

Chicago, Illinois

For information, address the publisher:
Raintree, 100 N. LaSalle, Suite 1200, Chicago, IL 60602

Customer Service: 888-363-4266
Visit our website at www.raintreelibrary.com

Printed and bound in China by South China Printing Company.
09 08 07 06 05
10 9 8 7 6 5 4 3 2 1

Library of Congress Cataloging-in-Publication Data:

Morris, Mark, 1965-
  Racing cars / Mark Morris.
    p. cm. -- (Mean machines)
  Includes bibliographical references and index.
  ISBN 1-4109-0556-X (lib. bdg., hardcover) -- ISBN 1-4109-0830-5 (pbk.) 1. Automobiles, Racing--Juvenile literature. I. Title. II. Series.
  TL236.M47 2004
  629.228--dc22
                              2004014132

Acknowledgments
Corbis 6, 14 (Michael Kim) 18, 20, 25 (Tempsport), 26 (Newsport), 30, 34–35 (Newsport), 36 (Newsport/George Tiedemann), 42 (David Read), 46 (Duomo), 46 (top) (Phillip Bailey), 53; Empics 10; Ferrari 5, 6, 7, 24, 27, 28; Giles Chapman 48; Honda 22 (bot), 22 (top), 27, 34, 38 (bot); Hulton-Getty 31, 33 (bot), 43, 52 (top), 52 (bot); Mirrorpix 47; PA Photos 4, 8, 41, 50 (top), 55 (top), 56; Rex Features 45; Science Photo Library 50, 55; Sutton Motorsport 9 (bot), 9 (top), 12, 13, 14 (bot), 16 (bot), 16 (top), 17, 18–19, 19, 20–21, 21, 23, 28, 29, 30, 32, 33 (top), 36, 37, 38 (top), 39, 40, 41 (bot), 41 (top), 44, 54, 56 (top); Th!nk 57.

Cover photograph of a Ferrari Formula 1 car reproduced with permission of Empics

Every effort has been made to contact copyright holders of any material reproduced in this book.
Any omissions will be rectified in subsequent printings if notice is given to the publishers.

Disclaimer
All the Internet addresses (URLs) given in this book were valid at the time of going to press. However, due to the dynamic nature of the Internet, some addresses may have changed, or sites may have changed or ceased to exist since publication. While the author and publisher regret any inconvenience this may cause readers, no responsibility for any such changes can be accepted by either the author or the publisher.

CONTENTS

Any words appearing in the text in bold,
like this, are explained in the glossary.
You can also look out for them in the "Up to
Speed" box at the bottom of each page.

THE NEED FOR SPEED

THE RIGHT CAR FOR THE RIGHT COURSE

Different kinds of races need different kinds of cars. The drivers have different skills, too. A Formula 1 Ferrari (see pages 28–29) might be hard to catch on a major race track, but it would not do too well in a hill climbing race!

The speed, danger, and excitement of auto racing have been with us for more than 100 years. For a century, drivers have pushed their machines to the limit, trying to beat everyone else. Everyone in auto racing has a simple dream: to go faster!

In the early days, a small number of people raced their unsafe machines to try to be the first across the line. Today, auto racing is a huge money-making industry. Thousands of people are involved. Drivers, mechanics, designers, engineers, and technicians give their all in the search for extra speed.

RACING EVERYWHERE

Auto racing comes in many shapes and sizes. Machines race around twisting tracks and **oval** circuits. They shoot across concrete and gravel. They zoom across ice, snow, and sandy deserts. Mud, dust, grass, and steep hills are all part of today's huge range of racing events.

Hundreds of thousands of spectators turn up to watch races. Millions more watch on television. Top racers are superstars and earn huge amounts of money. Everyone wants to win the exciting races. As long as cars exist, people will want to race them.

FIND OUT LATER . . .

When did racing cars weigh more than a ton?

Which is the fastest car on the planet?

Why do racing cars have "wings"?

THE RACING STORY

The early days of auto racing were a great adventure. People were excited by this new, fast-paced sport.

The cars were very different from those we see today. They were built high off the ground and looked very fragile. Some even had a "tiller" instead of a steering wheel. This is a stick that is normally used to steer small boats!

The engine was at the front of the car and the wheels and **chassis** were made from wood. Only three gears were normally used, and tires were often solid rubber. Engines today can be in the rear or middle of a racing car. Cars now have many more gears and much better tires.

EARLY HERO

Rene de Knyff was a successful early racing driver. He won the Paris to Bordeaux race in 1898. De Knyff was also involved in the creation of the Automobile Club de France, a major organization in the sport.

TECH TALK

Grand Prix Renault: technical data
- Engine size: 13 l (12,986 cc)
- Engine type: 4-**cylinder** in-line
- Engine power: 90 **hp**
- Top speed: 80 mph (128 km/h)

chassis   framework that supports a car's body
cylinder   tube-shaped part of an engine in which fuel is burned

EARLY DAYS AND DANGERS

There was very little protection for the driver and the passenger/mechanic. Ordinary clothes and thick goggles were their only defenses against wind, rain, snow, and flying stones. Early racers had to be tough. There were no safety belts. Some drivers thought it was safer to be thrown clear of a car if there was an accident.

The 1906 **Grand Prix** Renault is typical of racing cars from this time. Instead of being faster than its rivals, it had a good reputation for **reliability**. Problems could be fixed quicker than in other cars. It won because the other racers broke down!

THE GOOD OLD DAYS

Racing "classic" cars is a popular spectator event. People can admire the cars as well as enjoy a good race. The Goodwood Festival of Speed in England is an example of these meetings. It attracts thousands of race fans every year.

The Grand Prix Renault won the first ever Grand Prix in 1906.

hp (horse power)   measurement of engine power
reliability   ability to be trusted not to break down

7

THE WORLD'S BIGGEST RACES

In the very early days of auto racing, it was normal to race from one city to another. Gradually there was a move away from this to circuit racing. In circuit racing, cars go around the same track many times. The first "tracks" were public roads closed for the occasion. Then special race tracks were built.

There were a number of reasons for this change.

- City-to-city racing was dangerous. There were many accidents involving drivers and spectators.
- A special track could be made safer for spectators.
- At a track you can watch the whole race from start to finish.
- A track makes more money because spectators pay to watch.

LE MANS

The 8.5-mile (13.5-kilometer) track at Le Mans, France, is home to the Le Mans 24-hour **endurance** race. The teams of three drivers race thousands of miles through the day and night.

>>>>>>>>>>

Find out more about Le Mans on pages 40–41.

BIRTH OF THE BRICKYARD

The oldest track still in use today is the Indianapolis Motor Speedway. It was built in 1909 and is the home of the Indianapolis 500, one of the world's most famous races.

The track is a 2.5-mile (4-kilometer) **oval** circuit, nicknamed "the brickyard." The original track was made of 3.2 million bricks. Even though pavement now covers the original track, 36 inches (91 centimeters) of bricks are still in place at the finish line.

The cars that race are similar to Formula 1 cars (see pages 38–39), but bigger and more powerful. Around 250,000 fans come to watch each year.

SPEEDING THROUGH SPAIN
The Circuit di Catalunya, Spain, is one of the most exciting on the Formula 1 tour.

The "Indy 500" is 200 laps of this track.

DESIGN TECHNOLOGY

The engine of a racing car is complicated. *Very* complicated.

INCREDIBLE ENGINES

There are many moving parts that must work perfectly. **Valves** open and close many times every second. The fuel and air supply are carefully controlled. An exact amount of oil and water runs through the engine. Powerful computers manage all the workings of the engine.

The engine is often placed close behind the driver. This is done when top speeds need to be high. The front of the car can be lower, which makes it more **streamlined.** The car is easier to handle with most of the weight in the center.

TURBOCHARGERS

A turbocharger boosts engine power. A **turbine** is turned by **exhaust** fumes from the engine. The turbine powers a blower that forces the air back into the engine. This increases the mix of fuel and air, which improves the power.

fuel-injected   control of the fuel and air mixture in an engine
streamlined   designed to move easily through the air

FUEL INJECTION

Many racing car engines are **fuel-injected.** This is a way of controlling the mixture of fuel and air inside a **cylinder.** A computer figures out how much fuel is needed and when to inject it into the cylinder.

Very light metals, such as aluminum, are used to build racing engines. The engine must also be right for the car body that carries it. The most powerful engine is not always the best. There must be a balance between engine power and body structure.

This diagram shows how each piston in a four-stroke engine (see sidebar) works:

(see sidebar)

1. First down stroke.
   Air taken in.

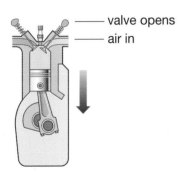

valve opens
air in

2. First up stroke.
   Fuel and air squeezed together.

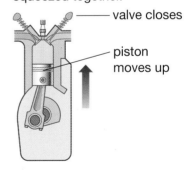

valve closes

piston moves up

3. Second down stroke.
   Mixture exploded by spark plug.

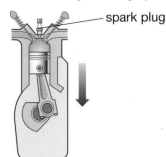

spark plug

4. Second up stroke.
   Exhaust fumes out.

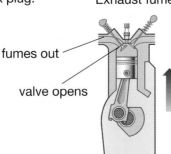

fumes out

valve opens

turbine fan that is turned by gas from an engine
valve allows movement of a fluid in one direction only

TIRES

Many people think that the tires are the most important part of a racing car. They are the only parts that come into contact with the track.

The tires must stay firmly on the road when the car **accelerates.** If they do not grip well, they will skid and the car will lose control.

Indy 500 and Formula 1 tires are very wide. This allows as much contact between rubber and track as possible. The front tires are slightly smaller, to cut down on **drag.**

HOT STUFF

Friction can make brakes heat up. Racing car brakes can glow red-hot. Disc brakes push pads against a disc that turns with the wheel. The disc can lose heat quickly. This is an advantage for a racing car, since the brakes stay working for longer.

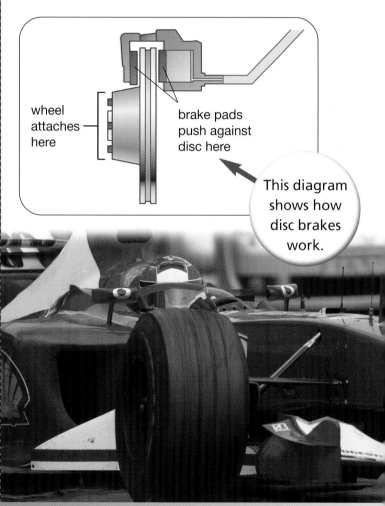

wheel attaches here

brake pads push against disc here

This diagram shows how disc brakes work.

TECH TALK

As a race goes on, the tires heat up. Racing tires can reach temperatures of 266 °F (130 °C).

accelerate   pick up speed and keep going faster
drag   force acting against something moving through air

KEEPING WARM

Racing tires grip better when they are warm. This is because the rubber softens as it warms up. Before a race starts, the tires are wrapped in special electric blankets. They are then already warm when the race starts and will grip better.

Drivers will swing their cars from side to side when driving up to the start line. This is another way of keeping the tires warm.

New tires fitted during a pit stop are kept in the special blankets. A driver will change to wet-weather tires if it rains. The tires used when it is dry are called slicks.

WET AND DRY

Slick tires for dry weather are not patterned. Wet-weather tires have a special pattern cut into them. The pattern helps to spread out water. This makes sure as much tire is in contact with the track as possible. Intermediate tires are between the two.

intermediate tires   wet-weather tires   slick tires

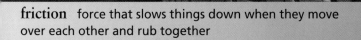

friction   force that slows things down when they move over each other and rub together

13

CHEATING THE WIND

Racing car designers are always searching for ways to make cars go faster. This does not always mean improving the engine. It can also mean improving the shape of a car. Designers try to make the car as sleek and **aerodynamic** as possible.

As a racing car speeds along, it has to cut through the air. A poor aerodynamic design creates **turbulence.** This increases the **drag** and slows the car down.

Racing cars are designed to make use of the airflow. When air hits the **wings** of a Formula 1 (see pages 38–39) or an Indy car, it pushes the car down. This keeps the car pressed to the track so it can corner more quickly.

WINGS AND GRIP

The wings on modern racing cars act like upside-down aircraft wings. An aircraft's wings create lift. Wings on a car create a downward force and give it a better grip.

aerodynamic   shape designed to move easily through the air
performance   how a vehicle functions and operates

WINGS

The first racing cars with wings appeared in 1968, such as the one in the picture below left. This was a big leap forward in **performance.**

Some racing machines even have air ducts at the front of the car. The air that rushes in presses the car to the track. The wings on the nose add to this effect.

The wings are adjustable and can be altered during a race if the conditions change.

A car that is not aerodynamic does not cut through the air well. This creates drag and limits its top speed.

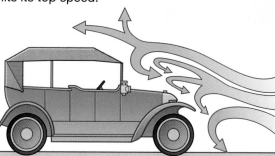

An aerodynamic racing car allows air to flow smoothly around it. This creates very little drag and the car can travel faster.

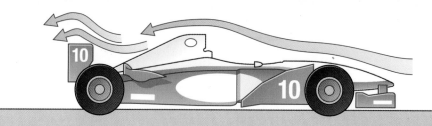

turbulence   rough, bumpy air flow around a car
wings   parts of a car that keep it stable at high speeds

Travelex

STRONG BUT LIGHT

Designers must use materials that are very light. This helps the car go as fast as possible without being weighed down. Materials such as Kevlar and **carbon fiber** are both very strong, but are much lighter than steel. The exhaust cover above is made from carbon fiber.

BUILDING A RACER

Designers are working hard to update racing cars. Teams of experts all have their own special jobs to do.

Modern computer technology means that engineers can test designs as **simulations.** This means they do not actually have to build them to test them out. Computer programs also help to build the cars to very high standards.

Thames Valley, England, is known internationally for its racing car building. Teams from all over the world go there to make use of the excellent engineers, designers, and mechanics in the area.

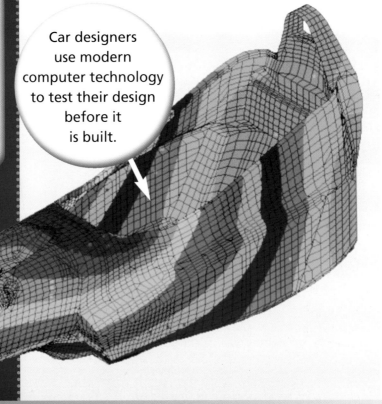

Car designers use modern computer technology to test their design before it is built.

carbon fiber   very hard, strong, light material

A YEAR IN THE LIFE OF A RACING CAR DESIGN TEAM

January
Building of the new car is finished.

December
Building of the new car begins.

February
The new car is tested. Areas for improvement go back to the designers.

November
Components are tested.

March
The new car is racing. Designers begin work on next year's improvements.

October
Other components are built.

April
New designs are computer-tested. Models are tested in a **wind tunnel**.

September
The new chassis is built.

May
The tests are looked at closely by engineers.

August
Building new **chassis components** starts.

June
The design of next year's car is drawn up.

July
A **prototype** is put through computer simulations.

A simple puncture can make even the best car undrivable.

TESTING CARS

Designers can test how new cars run without ever leaving the garage. They fix the cars to machines that copy the stress and strain of a real race. The team is able to avoid problems before they happen on the track.

prototype   test design built before the real thing is made
simulation   mock-up. A way of testing something without doing it for real.

17

SAFETY FIRST

Auto racing is dangerous. Even the world's greatest drivers are at risk. Ayrton Senna, a three-time Formula 1 World Champion, died in a crash in 1994. Great care must be taken to protect the drivers.

The safety of spectators is also very important. Many years ago there were some terrible accidents in which cars crashed into the stands. Today, spectators can watch a race in much safer surroundings.

Modern racing cars have a "survival cell." This is made of super-tough **carbon fiber** and makes the car's **cockpit** almost indestructible. Drivers are held in place by a **quick-release harness,** like those used by aircraft pilots.

JUST IN CASE . . .

Crash barriers and walls of rubber tires surround racing tracks. There are also **gravel traps** to slow cars down when they are out of control.

Around the track, **marshals** carry special fire equipment and can be at a crash in seconds. Cranes are also in place to lift damaged cars out of the way.

This woman will be protected in a crash by a roll hoop above her head.

cockpit   part of the car where the driver sits
gravel trap   large pit of gravel designed to slow a car down

RULES FOR SAFETY

Special rules are followed to reduce danger. Marshals wave flags to warn drivers about problems such as an accident. Sometimes a safety car is used to slow the race. The car is driven in front of the racers while any dangers are removed. Even though it is still very dangerous, racing is safer today than it has ever been.

FIRE CONTROL

Some cars carry special fire-control systems. These blanket the car in nitrogen if there is an accident. Special sensors inside the car trigger the nitrogen when fire is detected. This reduces the risk of the fuel tank exploding.

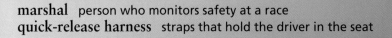

marshal   person who monitors safety at a race
quick-release harness   straps that hold the driver in the seat

IN THE DRIVER'S SEAT

Top drivers all have to start somewhere. Most of them learn to race in go-carts when they are young.

The small size of the carts makes them a great choice for new drivers. It is also cheap to race them. There are hundreds of different classes in which to race. The different classes mainly depend on engine size, the weight of the cart, the driver's age, and the type of fuel used.

The small carts are perfect for beginners. The biggest and quickest carts are different. They can reach 160 miles (256 kilometers) per hour.

RACING SCHOOL

All drivers must learn about their cars and their engines. They must also know race rules and emergency procedures. Understanding the car and its engine helps the driver to know just how fast and how aggressively to drive it.

In the early days of go-cart racing, old lawnmower engines were used.

GO-CARTS

Go-carts have very little bodywork. They will only have a front and rear bumper and two side panels. The engine is at the back, and the driver sits just in front of it. They are not very **aerodynamic.**

RACING LESSONS

Cart racing is fast and furious. The racers are usually bunched very closely together. They race around tracks about 0.5 miles (800 meters) long. Here the drivers learn all the skills they will need if they wish to race bigger cars in the future.

Formula Ford is another beginners' race class.

FORMULA FORD

Formula 1 World Champions Ayrton Senna, Nigel Mansell, Michael Schumacher, Mika Hakkinen, and James Hunt all launched their careers in Formula Ford racing.

TECH TALK

Typical go-cart: technical data
- Engine size: up to 0.25 l (250 cc)
- Engine type: 2- or 4-stroke
- Engine power: up to 80 **hp**
- Top speed: up to 160 **mph** (256 km/h)
- Weight: 430 lb (195 kg)
- Length: 6.9 ft (2.1 m)
- Width: 4.6 ft (1.4 m)

21

AT THE CONTROLS

The **cockpit** of a racing car is very strong. Even in a high-speed crash, it gives good protection. Since it is made of **carbon fiber,** it can also deal with very high temperatures.

Each cockpit is made to fit the driver. Cockpits are very tight and close-fitting. The driver has to squeeze inside, but this snug space holds him or her steady during a race. The seat is shaped to fit the driver's body shape exactly.

A racing driver has to cope with strong **G-forces** during a race. G-forces are the pressures felt by the driver when going around corners at a high speed. The perfect-fitting cockpit helps the driver cope with these pressures.

TIGHT FIT

The cockpits of Formula 1 and Indy cars are tight and close-fitting. The driver has to remove the steering wheel to get in and out of the car. The driver then replaces it when he or she is sitting inside.

G-force   force that acts on the driver in high-speed cornering

CONTROL INSTRUMENTS

At the driver's fingertips are the instruments that control the car. There are also instruments and dials to keep the driver informed about the car's **performance**.

There are special warning lights that tell the driver the perfect moment to change gear. There is no gear stick inside a cockpit, since it would make gear changes too slow. Instead, the driver can change gear in a fraction of a second by flicking special switches on the steering wheel. These switches are called **paddles.**

There are also controls to alter the fuel supply and a range of warning lights. The driver can even adjust the brakes while out on the track.

DEALING WITH GRAVITY

When racing drivers corner at high speeds, they are pushed sideways inside the car. This force can be five times stronger than the force of gravity. It is called the G-force. Drivers must be fit and strong to cope with this force.

Drivers must cope with strong G-forces, especially when they take corners.

DRESSED TO DRIVE

In the early days of racing, drivers wore ordinary clothes. If there was an accident, they had no protection. Things have changed a lot since then.

The biggest danger to a driver comes from fire. The **cockpit** of the car is very strong and can cope with heavy crashes. Racing cars carry **high-octane** fuel, however, which can quickly burst into flames.

Today, drivers are covered from head to toe in special clothing. The overall is made from a special material called Nomex.

Modern race helmets keep improving.

balaclava   tight-fitting mask that covers the whole head, with holes for mouth, nose, and eyes

FIRE FIGHTING

Under the overalls are more layers of protective clothing. Not everyone can claim that his or her underwear is fireproof! In fact, the clothes must protect the drivers from fire long enough to allow them to escape.

In addition to the long-sleeved top and full-length underwear, the driver also wears fireproof socks. A fireproof **balaclava** is worn under the helmet.

Some drivers wear four or five layers of this special protective clothing. Only the eyes are left uncovered. Unfortunately, this means the driver will be very hot underneath all the layers. Drivers can lose between 2.2 and 4.4 pounds (1–2 kilograms) in weight during a race because they sweat so much.

Nomex can cope with a fire of 1,292 °F (700 °C) for twelve seconds.

STRENGTH AND FITNESS

Racing drivers must be very fit. It takes strength to deal with the bumping and banging from the car. A lot of **endurance** and energy is needed to keep concentration and deal with the high temperature under the overalls and helmet.

high-octane powerful fuel that easily bursts into flames

PIT STOP

You might think a race team is just the driver and a few mechanics in the **pits.** They are the most visible on race days. Many more people are involved, though. A Formula 1 team can have up to 75 members.

All members of the team are highly trained. Vital time is lost when the car is in the pits, so it must get back to the track as quickly as possible.

PIT STOP SPEED

Formula 1 cars refill with fuel and change all their tires in about ten seconds! Pit mechanics spend many hours practicing. Even a small error could cost their car the race. A good pit stop can help to win a race.

TECH TALK

A Formula 1 team consists of:

- 6 tire mechanics
- 6 fuel mechanics
- 22 technicians to keep track of cars during races
- 5 spare-part managers
- 28 mechanics
- 5 drivers (including test drivers)
- 3 transportation managers

Total: 75 people

Grand Prix one of a series of major international auto races

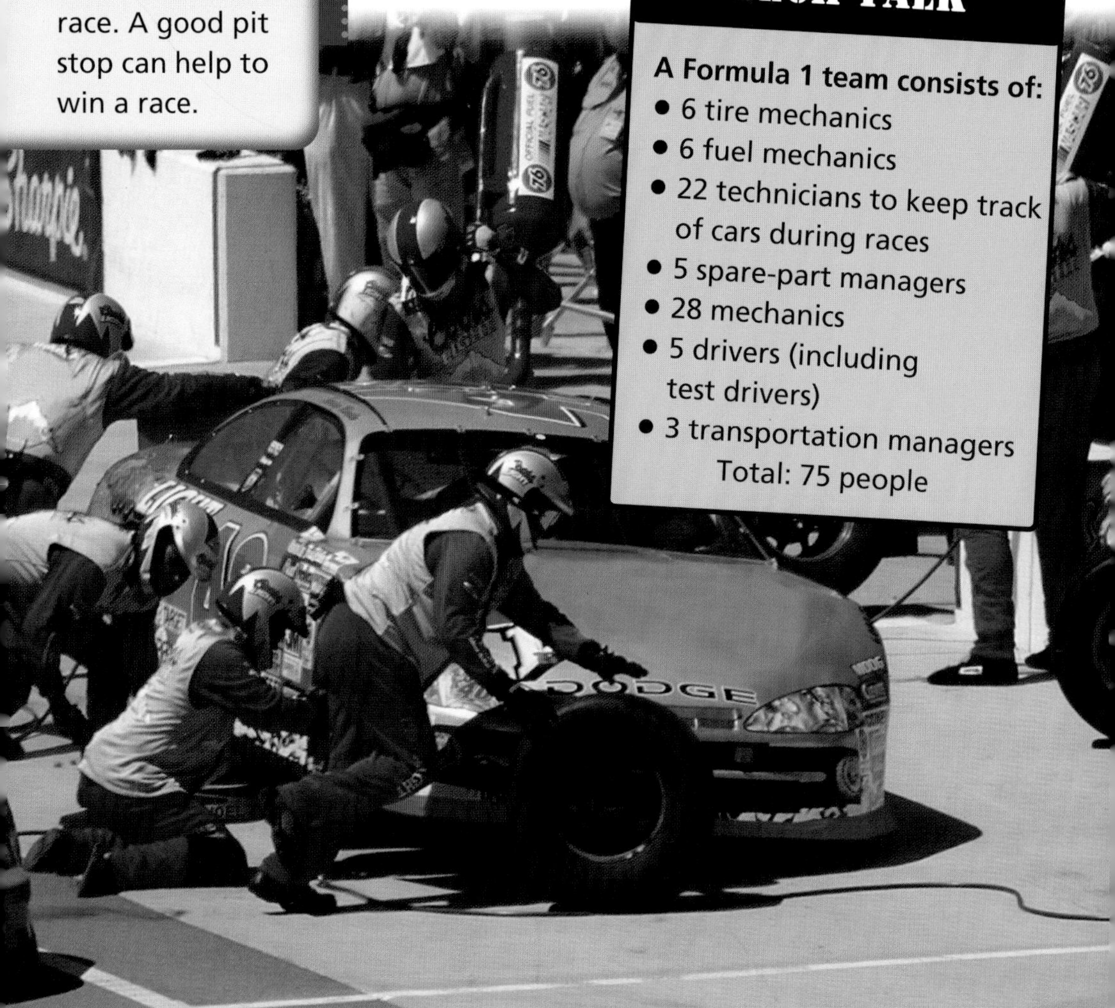

ACTION IN THE PITS

Pit stops are very exciting. When the car pulls in, mechanics will swarm around it like flies. It can look like chaos, but everyone knows his or her job, and they all rely on each other. Apart from refilling with fuel or changing tires, the mechanics might have to repair damaged bodywork.

During a race, the mechanics watch every part of the car and its **performance** with computer technology. Hundreds of **sensors** on the car keep track of everything. Even when it seems as though the driver is alone, there is still the help and support of the team.

Winning a **Grand Prix** is a team effort. Every top driver knows that success depends on the pit crew.

COMMUNICATION

The computer technicians may see a potential problem when the car is out on the race track. They can still help by sending this information straight to the driver's helmet over a hi-tech radio system.

During a pit stop, the crew has just a few seconds to change the tires and refuel the car.

---

pits where cars stop for fuel and repairs during a race
sensor electronic device that receives signals and responds to them

CARS AND DRIVERS

The Italian car-maker Ferrari produces some of the world's best racing cars. There have been many excellent machines painted in its world-famous red colors.

FERRARI FROM ABOVE

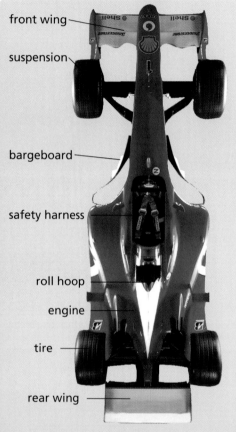

front wing

suspension

bargeboard

safety harness

roll hoop

engine

tire

rear wing

FANTASTIC FERRARI

Ferraris have won at Le Mans (see pages 40–41) many times and are the most successful builders of Formula 1 cars to date. Ferrari has also had some famous Formula 1 champions. Alberto Ascari won for Ferrari twice in the 1950s and John Surtees won in the 1960s. The 1970s saw the legendary Nikki Lauda become world champion for Ferrari as well as Jody Scheckter. More recently, Michael Schumacher has dominated Formula 1 racing for Ferrari.

UP TO SPEED World Constructors' Championship Competition that rewards the best car over a Formula 1 racing season

THE ONE TO BEAT

The Ferrari in the pictures won the **World Constructor's Championship** in 2000. It combines the most up-to-date design features with an awesome engine.

Ferrari prides itself on building the whole machine—the body as well as the engine. Some companies, such as Honda, only make engines for Formula 1 racing. Then they form a partnership with a racing team that builds the body.

Even people who are not interested in auto racing know how successful Ferraris are.

THE FIRST RACES

The first official car race was in 1895. Five cars took part and the winner managed a speed of 9.6 mph (15.4 km/h)! There have been huge changes since then.

The French began to hold races over long distances of 750 miles (1,200 kilometers). The first was from Paris to Bordeaux and back. The cars were so hard to drive, the drivers took mechanics along with them.

City-to-city racing gradually stopped, and specially built tracks sprang up. Racers wanted more power, so cars had huge engines. Cars of the time weighed more than a ton.

BRILLIANT BENTLEY

Cars built by the company Bentley became a legend at Le Mans, the 24-hour speed and **endurance race**. This 4.5-liter (4,500-cc) car was known as the Blower Bentley and broke the **lap record** in 1930 at nearly 87 mph (140 km/h).

This Alfa-Romeo won the first ever World Driver's Championship in 1950.

lap record   fastest time anyone has taken to do a single lap of a race track; each track has its own record

GRAND PRIX PEUGEOT

The car manufacturer Peugeot started a trend toward smaller, lighter cars. Peugeot saw that the power of the engine was only one factor in winning a race.

The **Grand Prix** Peugeot was built in 1912. It was designed by Ernest Henry and was driven by Georges Boillot and Jules Goux, who were also the engineers. This classic vehicle is the great-grandfather of all modern racing cars. It beat cars with engines twice its size. The Peugeot was lighter, so its smaller engine did not have so much weight to carry.

Boillot became the first man to win two Grands Prix in this car and became a national hero. The car also won the Indianapolis 500 in 1913, driven by Goux.

IMPROVING DESIGNS

As the 20th century went on, racing cars became more sophisticated. Engineers moved the driver's seat to the center of the **cockpit.** This meant they could change the cockpit's overall design, making it more **streamlined.**

Engineers also developed the **monocoque chassis.** This is a single structure that is the skeleton of the car. Old chassis types had the body built on to them, so that many pieces were joined together. The monocoque is a single part. This means that it is stronger and lighter.

Turbochargers, supercharged engines, and electronic systems were slowly introduced. Braking systems, tires, and streamlining were all improved. The racing car became much closer to what we recognize today.

SETTING THE STANDARD

The Lotus-Climax 25 in the picture below broke new ground in racing car design. The monocoque chassis and improved **suspension** systems are basically still used today. Designers agree that the car was a turning point in modern racing car design.

Jim Clark won the World Championship in this car in 1963. He won seven of the ten races that year.

TECH TALK

Lotus-Climax 25: technical data
- Engine size: 1.5 l (1,500 cc)
- Engine type: V8 **cylinder** Coventry-Climax
- Engine power: 195 **hp**
- Top speed: 150 mph (240 km/h)

Lotus began an impressive history with this car. They won a total of 79 **Grand Prix** races.

FERRARI SUCCESS

The 2000 Ferrari (above) won back the World Drivers' Championship for Ferrari after a gap of twenty years. Michael Schumacher won nine of the seventeen races in that year. He won again in 2001, 2002, and 2003.

suspension   system that keeps the body of a car still while the wheels go over dips and bumps in the road surface

SPONSORS

Auto racing is a very glamorous sport that attracts much attention. Large crowds of people go to races, and many watch on television.

Big companies see auto racing as a way of linking themselves with something exciting. They sign deals with the racing teams and give them money. In return, the teams display the company's name on their racing cars. These deals are called **sponsorship**.

SPONSORS EVERYWHERE

The race teams use every possible opportunity to get funding for the team. Even the drivers' overalls are covered in sponsors' badges and logos.

Many different companies sponsor auto racing. Some, like oil and gasoline companies, have obvious reasons for wanting their name on a winning car. Clothing companies, television stations, and sports manufacturers all sponsor auto racing, too.

RAISING MONEY

Auto racing is a very expensive sport. Racing teams need huge amounts of money every year. Sponsorship is an important way of raising money for racing teams. Without the money of the sponsors, auto racing would be in serious trouble.

The logos of the sponsors are all over racing cars. The bigger the logo, the more the company will have paid to the race team. All around the race track there is more advertising and sponsorship. When television interviews are done before and after the race, the background will be covered in logos. When the winner of a race collects the trophy, even the **podium** will have sponsors' badges on it.

AUTO RACING SPONSORS

Here are a few of the companies that have sponsored auto racing:

- Coca-Cola
- Home Depot
- Benetton
- McDonald's
- Ford Motor Co.
- Shell
- Hewlett-Packard
- Cheerios
- Total
- Kodak

sponsorship giving money for an activity in return for advertising. The advertiser is called the sponsor.

THE WORLD OF RACING

If the cars in a race are alike, the action will be fast and furious. Crashes are more likely, and only a few cars are likely to finish the race.

OVAL TRACK RACERS

The National Association for Stock Car Racing (NASCAR) holds races around **oval** tracks. The cars look like **production cars,** but they have much bigger and more powerful engines.

The cars have many safety features, since crashes happen often in stock car racing. They have special safety flaps on the roof that stand up if the car spins. When upright, the flaps spoil the **streamlined** shape of the car and stop it from lifting off the ground. The cars shoot around the oval track at up to 200 mph (320 km/h).

NASCAR SAFETY

The **roll hoop** of a NASCAR is super-strong. In NASCAR racing the tracks are tight, so the cars bunch together. This means that accidents and crashes are common. The car windows are covered with nylon netting to stop wreckage from getting inside during a crash.

production car   car built in large numbers for general sale. These are the everyday cars that anyone can own and drive

ACTION-PACKED

An oval track has a big advantage for spectators. They are able to see the whole race. Since the cars are close together, oval tracks have plenty of excitement. Cars often hit each other. Cars will even deliberately nudge each other to gain an advantage in a corner.

FAST CORNERING

On a flat track, fast cornering can lead to a car sliding off the track. Oval tracks with banked corners that slope upward, allow cars to go faster around them. This is because the banking acts against the **G-forces** created by the turn.

TECH TALK

Typical NASCAR stock car: technical data
- Engine size: 5.8 l (5,800 cc)
- Engine type: V8
- Engine power: 700 h p
- Top speed: 200 mph (320 km/h)
- Weight: 3,300 lb (1,500 kg)

The banked corners of a NASCAR track mean that the cars can take corners quickly.

DIFFERENT FORMULAS

Racing in cars with only a single seat is split up into different classes. These classes are called formulas.

The "formula" is a list of rules about the size of a racing car, its engine power, weight, and design.

FORMULA 3000

In 1985 Formula 2 was replaced by Formula 3000. The name comes from the 3,000-cc (3-liter) engines used. Formula 3000 is now seen as the last step before the big prize—a drive in a top Formula 1 car.

The formulas make sure that races are exciting, because all the competing cars are similar to each other. Drivers can learn their skills in the lesser formula races, such as Formula Ford, Formula 3, and Formula 3000. If a driver is successful, one day he or she might get a chance to race in the best machines: Formula 1.

To race in Formula 1 is the ultimate challenge.

SINGLE-SEAT INTERNATIONAL RACING: THE BASIC RULES

Formula Ford

This is a beginners' class of racing. The cars are all powered by the same engines. They have similar designs to a Formula 1 car, but without **wings**.

Formula 3

This is another beginners' formula, but for more experienced drivers who want to get to the top. The cars have more power and they also have wings.

Formula 2 or Formula 3000

This class is for serious drivers trying to break into Formula 1 racing. The cars are very similar to Formula 1 cars, but with only two-thirds of the power.

Formula 1

The top of the tree. There are still rules about how big an engine can be and also about the design. Cars reach speeds of up to 225 miles (360 kilometers) per hour.

FORMULA 3

Famous drivers such as Jackie Stewart, Mika Hakkinen, Rubens Barrichello, Nelson Piquet, and Emerson Fittipaldi have all been Formula 3 champions.

Many of the best Formula 1 drivers learned their skills driving in Formula 3.

39

ENDURANCE RACING

An **endurance** race is not just about speed. The winners must cover the greatest distance in a certain time. The two most famous races are held at Le Mans in France and in Sebring, Florida. Successful endurance racing cars must have great **performance** and **reliability.** Without these, they will never win at Le Mans or Sebring.

LE MANS

The first Le Mans race was held in 1923, and this 24-hour race is loaded with glamour, style, and tradition. Until 1969, drivers had to run across the track to their cars when the race started. Now they have a **rolling start.**

THE LE MANS TRACK

Originally the Le Mans course was nearly 11 miles (17.5 kilometers) long. Over the years, alterations have been made. The track is now just under 8.5 miles (13.5 kilometers). Many race fans believe it is the best track in the world.

rolling start   race start in which cars slowly drive behind a marshal's car before the marshall turns away and the race begins

SEBRING

Endurance races began at Sebring, Florida, in 1952. The car furthest ahead after twelve hours is the winner. Races at Sebring are famous for excitement and close finishes.

AUDI ENDURANCE

Cars that race at Le Mans and Sebring have to be tough as well as fast. The Audi R8 dominated the 2000, 2001, and 2002 Le Mans races. In 2002 it broke the **lap record** by more than four seconds. The winning car also set a new record for the distance covered of 375 laps.

NIGHT DRIVING

The drivers race in shifts right through the night at Le Mans. Driving at high speeds in the dark is dangerous. The drivers must stay alert and keep their concentration.

TECH TALK

2003 Audi R8: technical data
- Engine size: 3.6 l (3,600 cc)
- Engine type: V8 turbocharged
- Engine power: 610 h p
- Top speed: 200 mph (320 km/h)
- Weight: 2,000 lb (906 kg)
- Fuel tank size: 24 gal (90 l)

There is no comfortable pavement track for rally cars. Rally cars go everywhere and drive in terrible conditions. They race on concrete, gravel, grass, snow, ice, and mud.

Although they look similar to **production cars,** underneath there are big differences. The engines are highly tuned and racing gears are fitted. The cars are fitted with many extra safety features, which make them super-tough. **Four-wheel drive** is used, since this gives the best grip in all weather conditions.

The best rally cars are **all-arounders.** They are quick on straight courses, can corner sharply, and can cope with the shocks and bumps.

MONTE CARLO RALLY

The Monte Carlo rally is the most famous of all. It is extremely tough, and the weather conditions play a big part. In 1965 only 22 cars out of 237 managed to finish. The picture below shows the eventual winner in 1965, the Mini-Cooper "S."

TECH TALK

Audi Quattro S1: technical data
- Engine size: 2.1 l (2,110 cc)
- Engine type: 5 **cylinders** in-line
- Engine power: 444 **h p**
- Weight: 2,650 lb (1,200 kg)
- Top speed: 155 **mph** (248 km/h)

all-arounder   good at a number of different things
four-wheel drive   vehicle with all wheels turned by the engine

TEAM WORK

The cars are designed to be taken apart quickly. This is so that repairs can be made as quickly as possible. Even major engine parts such as the gearbox can be replaced in as little as fifteen minutes.

Rally cars carry a driver and a **navigator.** While the driver concentrates hard on the course, the navigator shouts instructions over the intercom. They work together as a team.

The Peugeot 206 WRC has been a very successful rally car in recent years.

TECH TALK

Peugeot 206 WRC: technical data
- Engine size: 2 l (1,997 cc)
- Engine power: 300 h p
- Weight: 2,700 lb (1,230 kg)
- Top speed: 135 mph (216 km/h)

DESERT STORMERS

There are a number of famous desert races around the world.

The Baja 500 is a very popular race for many types of vehicle. They race in different classes. Even motorcycles take part. It starts and finishes in Ensenada, Mexico, with 500 miles (800 kilometers) across the Baja desert in between.

The Australian Safari is another very popular desert race. Competitors race across extreme desert conditions. The course changes each year, but Darwin to Sydney has been one of the most popular routes. Again, there are different classes for different vehicle types.

PARIS TO DAKAR

The Paris to Dakar is probably the most famous desert race. It begins on Christmas Day (December 25) and lasts right into January. The riders have to cross the Sahara desert in twenty days. They race over 13,000 miles (20,800 kilometers).

TOUGH CONDITIONS

Cars that race across the desert have to be tough. The bumpy conditions mean they often end up upside down on their roofs. The driver and **navigator** sit inside a super-strong **roll hoop.** This stops the roof from crushing them if the car flips over.

The car also has to cope with all the rocks and bumps the desert can throw at it. The **suspension** must be excellent. The tires have a special chunky pattern that gives extra grip.

All the mechanical parts have to deal with a terrible enemy: sand. It gets everywhere and can ruin an engine very quickly. Desert racers have engines that protect against this problem.

These vehicles can go almost anywhere!

DRAGSTERS

Drag racing is the fastest of all motor sports. The cars, called dragsters, handle very badly and cannot even take corners. They are only designed to do one thing—**accelerate** faster than anything on Earth!

Top dragsters do not burn gasoline. They use a special fuel called nitromethane.

Dragsters race on a straight track that is only .25 miles (400 meters) long. Two cars race at a time. The top cars leave the starting line faster than a jet aircraft. They reach 100 mph (160 km/h) in less than a second.

The engines are so powerful that the ground shakes when they start. The noise is deafening, but the excitement is awesome, even though the races only last for a few seconds.

DRAGSTER FUEL

Nitromethane is a very powerful fuel and has to be handled carefully. It can produce a gas called nitric acid, which is powerful enough to eat through metal.

This dragster is doing a "burn-out."

wheelie bar   bar that extends from the back of a dragster; it stops it from flipping over backward when accelerating

SPEED DEMONS

Dragsters are hard to control. They have so much power that the front of a car lifts off the ground when it accelerates. To stop them from flipping right over, a **wheelie bar** is fitted to the rear.

Drivers warm up their tires before races by doing "burn-outs." This is because warm tires grip better than cold ones. With the brakes firmly on, they rev the engine hard. Clouds of thick, black smoke bellow out. **Friction** between the tires and ground warms up the tires.

The top dragsters can reach speeds of 320 mph (512 km/h). Racing a dragster is more like hanging on to a rocket than driving a car!

SLOWING DOWN

The fastest dragsters cannot rely on their brakes to stop them. Their incredibly high speeds mean they must release a parachute to bring them to a halt. Jet aircraft use similar parachutes when they land on aircraft carriers.

HILL CLIMBS

Pikes Peak is in the Rocky Mountains in Colorado. It can be seen from hundreds of miles away and has inspired people for thousands of years. It also inspires racing drivers. Every year a special race is held there: the Pikes Peak International Hill Climb.

The race is the second oldest in the United States. Only the Indianapolis 500 is older. Rea Lentz was the first winner in 1916. His time was 20 minutes and 55.6 seconds.

There are many different race classes. Sports cars, stock cars, trucks, and motorcycles all race their way to the top. There are even running races for athletes.

Rod Millen driving his Toyota Tacoma at high speed up Pikes Peak.

STAYING ON THE ROAD

The course is very dangerous. The cars can reach over 130 miles (208 kilometers) per hour on the narrow straights of the twisting road. There are 156 gravel turns that kick up huge clouds of dust. There are also the cliffs to worry about. There are no barriers or guard rails around the course. Just a sheer drop of 2,000 feet (600 meters).

TECH TALK

Pikes Peak: course information
- Length: 12.42 mi (20 km)
- Surface: gravel
- Starting height: 9,200 ft (2,805 m)
- Finishing height: 14,100 ft (4,301 m)
- Track width: straights 19.7 ft (6 m), corners 19.7–49.2 ft (6–15 m)

PIKES PEAK RECORDS

- Most wins: Louis Unser: 9
- Most wins in a row: Bobby Unser: 6
- Most new records set: Bobby Unser: 7

The race was invented as a way to encourage the use of the road through the mountains. Today it is legendary and one of the world's top classic races.

The route of the Pikes Peak race.

Summit
Boulder Park
Bottomless Pit
Double Cut
Devil's Playground
Elk Park
Race to the Clouds Starting Line
Brown Bush Corner
Glen Cove Food and Rest Stop
Blue Sky
Halfway Picnic Ground

RACE IN THE SUN

The World Solar Challenge is a special race for cars powered only by the sun. Many believe that this technology will one day power all vehicles in the future.

The race takes place across Australia and was first held in 1987. The first winner was the *Sunraycer*, with an average speed of 41.9 miles (67 kilometers) per hour.

SUNSHARK

The *Sunshark* managed to compete with machines that had cost millions of dollars to develop. The *Sunshark* cost only $15,000. Its average speed during the 1996 race was 40.6 mph (65 km/h).

TECH TALK

The *Sunraycer* did not just win the first Solar Challenge; it beat everyone out of sight. The second-place vehicle was more than 600 miles (960 kilometers) behind when the *Sunraycer* finished!

Sunraycer's record for the fastest winning time was broken in 1993. The winning car traveled 499 miles (803 kilometers) in a single day.

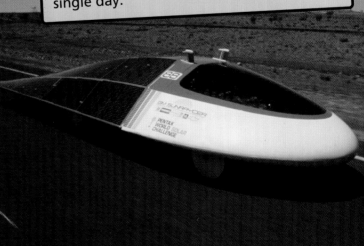

amateur   someone who does not get paid for what he or she is doing. Professionals do get paid.

RACING FOR THE FUTURE

The race is now held each year between Darwin and Adelaide. The vehicles that take part look like something from a science-fiction movie.

Huge companies spend millions **sponsoring** some of the competitors. Other teams come from colleges or are groups of **amateurs.**

All those who take part are not just competing in a race. They are helping to develop technology for the future. Oil and gasoline will not last forever because the earth only has so much. It is important that we make cars for the future.

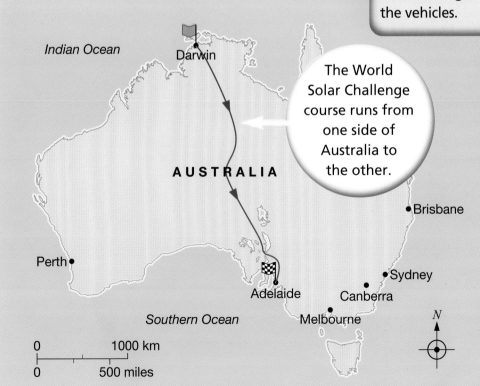

Indian Ocean

Darwin

The World Solar Challenge course runs from one side of Australia to the other.

AUSTRALIA

•Brisbane

Perth•

•Sydney

Adelaide

Canberra

Southern Ocean

Melbourne

N

0   1000 km

0   500 miles

ULTIMATE RACERS

The name *Bluebird* is a legend in speed record breaking. Sir Malcolm Campbell broke the land-speed record nine times. Every car he drove was called *Bluebird*. Sir Malcolm also broke the water-speed record three times.

In the 1960s his son, Donald Campbell, tried to follow in his father's footsteps. The car was also called *Bluebird*.

In 1960 Donald Campbell tried to reach 400 mph (640 km/h), but there was a bad crash. The car flipped into the air and turned over four times before hitting the ground. Campbell cracked his skull and nearly died.

ELECTRIC SPEED

In 1899 Camille Jenatzy broke the land-speed record in a car powered by electricity. He reached the speed 65.8 mph (105.3 km/h). This was the world's first car that was designed to do only one thing: go faster than anything else at the time.

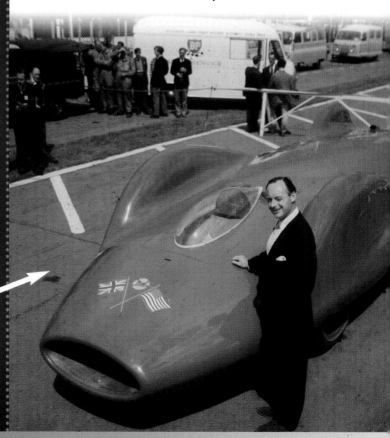

Bluebird's engine would blow itself apart after three minutes at full speed!

CHASING RECORDS, NOT DRIVERS

Donald Campbell would not give up. By 1964 the car was rebuilt. He was ready to try again. The car was taken to Australia and this time he was successful. The car reached 403 mph (645 km/h).

Donald had followed his father into history. Unfortunately Donald died in 1967 when trying to break the water-speed record. His boat was also called *Bluebird*.

TECH TALK

Land-speed records: the rules
- The course must be driven twice in opposite directions.
- The average speed of the two runs is taken for the record.
- Both runs must be done in under one hour.

SUPERSONIC

The *Thrust SSC* is an incredible car. SSC stands for SuperSonic Car. In 1997 it set a new land-speed record of 763 miles (1,221 kilometers) per hour. It is the only car to go faster than the speed of sound.

An expert on rockets and guided missiles designed the car. It was driven by Andy Green, a former jet pilot in Britain's Royal Air Force.

NOBLE OWNER

Richard Noble owns *Thrust SSC*. He broke the land-speed record in 1983 in a car called *Thrust 2*. His record stood for fourteen years. Noble did not drive *Thrust SSC* himself because he was not used to traveling at supersonic speeds.

TECH TALK

Thrust SSC: **technical data**
- **Engines:** Rolls-Royce Spey 202s from Phantom jet fighters
- **Weight:** 11 tons
- **Acceleration:** 0–100 mph (0–160 km/h) in four seconds; 0–600 mph (0–960km/h) in sixteen seconds

THRUSTING ON

Andy Green set off on the first attempt. The **sound barrier** was broken. Everyone there heard the deafening **sonic boom.** But the car went too far past the finishing marker. They had one hour to turn around for the next run. They took 61 minutes. They were fast enough, but they broke the rules. The first record attempt had failed.

They set off again and there were no problems. They smashed the record!

The record was broken in the Black Rock Desert, Nevada. The run was on a dry lake bed that was 19 miles (30 kilometers) long. This is one of very few places on Earth that is right for a record attempt.

DOUBLE THE POWER

Thrust SSC has state-of-the-art technology and is the only jet car to have two engines.

The *Thrust SSC* has the same power as 1,000 family cars or 145 Formula 1 racing cars.

FUTURE RACERS

So what will the racing cars of the future be like?

It seems likely that new fuels will be used, because one day oil and gasoline will run out. General Motors has produced a **prototype** fuel cell car. The car runs on hydrogen.

NEW FUELS

Perhaps the future will see new fuels. Team Nasamax has designed a Cosworth engine that runs on **bio-ethanol**. This fuel is made from waste agricultural products and does not produce the **exhaust** fumes of normal fuel.

Having a new fuel means that many other things may change. The fuel cell could be put into a normal vehicle, but it does not need the same space as an old engine. The driver would not have to look out over an engine any more.

GM's *AUTOnomy*, pictured below, has a very low **chassis,** and the fuel cells are contained inside it. There is no need for an engine space.

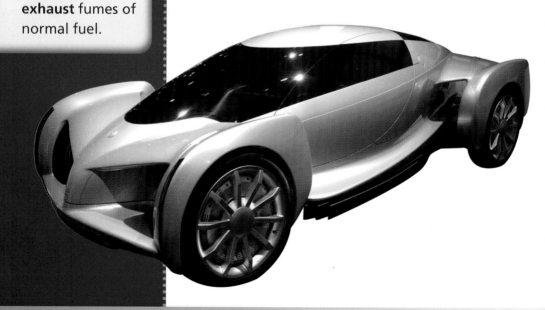

bio-ethanol   fuel made from waste products. It does not produce the same harmful gases as other fuels.

STARTING OVER

Designers can throw away the rule book and start from scratch. The space left by the engine could now be filled with safety features to protect the driver in an accident.

Because all the technology is in the chassis, GM's *AUTOnomy* has been nicknamed the "skateboard on steroids." The makers suggest that a driver could own one chassis and several different bodies. These could be swapped around for different needs.

Braking, steering, and **acceleration** information are carried by wires rather than a **steering column** and mechanical levers. This means the driver could sit anywhere, even in the back.

NEW THINKING

This car is powered by electricity. It has a range of about 60 miles (95 kilometers) after a single charge. A recharge can be done overnight at home and is very cheap.

X677 YOO

Cars of the future are going to be very different from the ones we have now.

exhaust   pipe that releases waste gases from the engine
steering column   device that links the steering wheel to the wheels

RACING CAR FACTS

The history of the land-speed record				
			Speed	
Date	**Driver**	**Car**	**Mph**	**km/h**
1909	Victor Héméry	*Benz No. 1*	115.9	186.5
1924	Malcolm Campbell	*Sunbeam Bluebird*	146.2	235.3
1926	Henry Segrave	*Sunbeam Ladybird*	149.3	240.4
1927	Henry Segrave	*Sunbeam Slug*	203.8	328.0
1932	Malcolm Campbell	*CNR Bluebird*	254.0	408.8
1935	Malcolm Campbell	*CR-RR Bluebird*	301.1	484.6
1938	John Cobb	*Railton*	350.2	563.6
1963	Craig Breedlove	*Spirit of America*	407.4	655.6
1964	Craig Breedlove	*Spirit of America*	526.3	847.0
1965	Craig Breedlove	*Spirit of America – Sonic 1*	600.6	966.6
1970	Gary Gabelich	*Blue Flame*	622.4	1001.7
1983	Richard Noble	*Thrust 2*	633.5	1019.5
1997	Andy Green	*Thrust SSC*	763.0	1227.9

Fastest production cars		
Car	**Speed**	
Bugatti 16/4 Veyron	252 mph	406 km/h
Koenigsegg CC	240 mph	386 km/h
McLaren F1	231 mph	372 km/h
Saleen S7	220 mph	354 km/h
Jaguar XJ220	220 mph	354 km/h
Ferrari Enzo	217 mph	350 km/h
Bugatti EB110 GT	212 mph	341 km/h
Lamborghini Diablo 6.0	210 mph	338 km/h
Lamborghini Murciélago	205 mph	330 km/h
Ferrari F40	202 mph	325 km/h

Quickest to 60 mph (100 km/h)	
Car	**Time**
Bugatti 16/4 Veyron	3.0 s
McLaren F1	3.2 s
Caterham 7 Superlight R500	3.4 s
Westfield 317 FW400	3.5 s
Lamborghini Murciélago	3.7 s
Ferrari F50	3.7 s
Ferrari Enzo	3.7 s
TVR Tuscan 4.5	3.8 s
Noble M12 GTO3	3.9 s
Dodge Viper SRT-10	3.9 s

There are around 400 million cars in the world. By 2020 there will probably be around one billion.

Formula 1 world champions since 1994		IndyCar world champions since 1994	
Year	**Driver**	**Year**	**Driver**
1994	Michael Schumacher	1994	Al Unser Jr.
1995	Michael Schumacher	1995	Jacques Villeneuve
1996	Damon Hill	1996	Jimmy Vasser
1997	Jacques Villeneuve	1997	Alex Zanardi
1998	Mika Hakkinen	1998	Alex Zanardi
1999	Mika Hakkinen	1999	Juan Montoya
2000	Michael Schumacher	2000	Gil de Ferran
2001	Michael Schumacher	2001	Gil de Ferran
2002	Michael Schumacher	2002	Christiano da Matta
2003	Michael Schumacher	2003	Paul Tracy

The first motorist to be arrested for speeding in the United Staes was pulled over by a policeman on a bicycle. It was 1899, and the driver of the car was going 12 mph (19 km/h)!

FIND OUT MORE

BOOKS

Baukus Mello, Tara. *Need for Speed*. Broomall, Penn.: Chelsea House, 2000.

Cefrey, Holly. *Race Car Drivers: Life on the Fast Track*. New York: Rosen, 2001.

Stewart, Mark. *Dale Earnhardt, Jr.: Driven by Destiny*. Brookfield, Conn.: Millbrook, 2003.

WORLD WIDE WEB

If you want to find out more about cars, you can search the Internet using keywords such as these:

- "land-speed record"
- rally + cars
- dragsters

Make your own keywords using headings or words from this book.

WEB SITES

NASCAR
Catch up on the latest news, statistics, and pictures about NASCAR.
nascar.com

INDIANAPOLIS 500
This site is full of information, statistics, and news about this famous race.
indy500.com

SEARCH TIPS

There are billions of pages on the Internet, so it can be difficult to find exactly what you want to find. If you just type in "car" on a search engine such as Google, you will get a list of millions of web pages. These search skills will help you find useful websites more quickly.

- Use simple keywords, not whole sentences.
- Use two to six keywords in a search.
- Be precise—only use names of people, places, or things.
- If you want to find words that go together, put quote marks around them—for example "world-speed record."
- Use the advanced section of your search engine.
- Use the "+" sign between keywords to find pages with all these words.

GLOSSARY

accelerate pick up speed and keep going faster

aerodynamic shape designed to move easily through the air

all-arounder good at a number of different things

amateur someone who does not get paid for what he or she is doing. Professionals get paid.

balaclava tight-fitting mask that covers the whole head, with holes for mouth, nose, and eyes

bio-ethanol fuel made from waste products. It does not produce the same harmful gases as other fuels.

carbon fiber very hard, strong, light material

chassis framework that supports a car's body

cockpit part of the car where the driver sits, normally a single-seater

cylinder tube-shaped part of an engine in which fuel is burned

drag force acting against something moving through air

endurance ability to survive long and stressful conditions

exhaust pipe that releases waste gases from the engine

four-wheel drive vehicle that has all four wheels turned directly by the engine

friction force that slows things down when they move over each other and rub together

fuel-injection highly accurate control of the fuel and air mixture in an engine

G-force force that acts on the driver in high-speed cornering

Grand Prix one of a series of major international auto races

gravel trap large pit of gravel designed to slow a car down

high-octane powerful fuel that easily bursts into flames

hp (horse power) a measurement of engine power

lap record fastest time anyone has taken to do a single lap of a track. Each track has its own record.

marshal person who monitors safety at a race

monocoque single-piece chassis

navigator person who guides the driver across a route

oval egg-shaped

paddles small switches on a steering wheel for changing gear

performance how a vehicle functions and operates; the speed, braking, cornering, and so on

piston sits inside the cylinder and moves backward and forward

pits where cars stop for fuel and repairs during a race

podium place on which the winning trophy is presented

production car car built in large numbers for general sale. These are the everyday cars that anyone can own and drive.

prototype test design built before the real thing is made

quick-release harness straps that hold the driver in the seat. The straps can be released by pressing a button.

reliability ability to be trusted not to break down

roll hoop strong framework built into a car to protect the driver if the car rolls over

rolling start race start in which the cars drive slowly in order behind a marshal's car before it turns away and the race begins

sensor electronic device that receives signals and responds to them

simulation mock-up; a way of testing something without doing it for real

sonic boom noise heard when a vehicle passes by at a speed faster than the speed of sound

sound barrier drag and other problems that make a vehicle hard to control when it gets close to the speed of sound

sponsorship giving money for an activity in return for advertising. The advertiser is called the sponsor.

steering column device that links the steering wheel to the wheels

streamlined designed to move easily through the air

suspension system that keeps the body of a car still while the wheels go over dips and bumps in the road surface

turbine fan that is turned by gas from an engine

turbulence rough, bumpy air flow around a car

valve allows movement of a fluid in one direction only

wheelie bar bar that extends from the back of a dragster. It stops the dragster from flipping over backward when accelerating.

wings parts of a car that keep it stable at high speeds

World Constructors' Championship Competition that rewards the best car over a Formula 1 racing season

INDEX